Young Gypsies

Our lives, culture and traditions

CL11 TF (P)   PSL 1827A

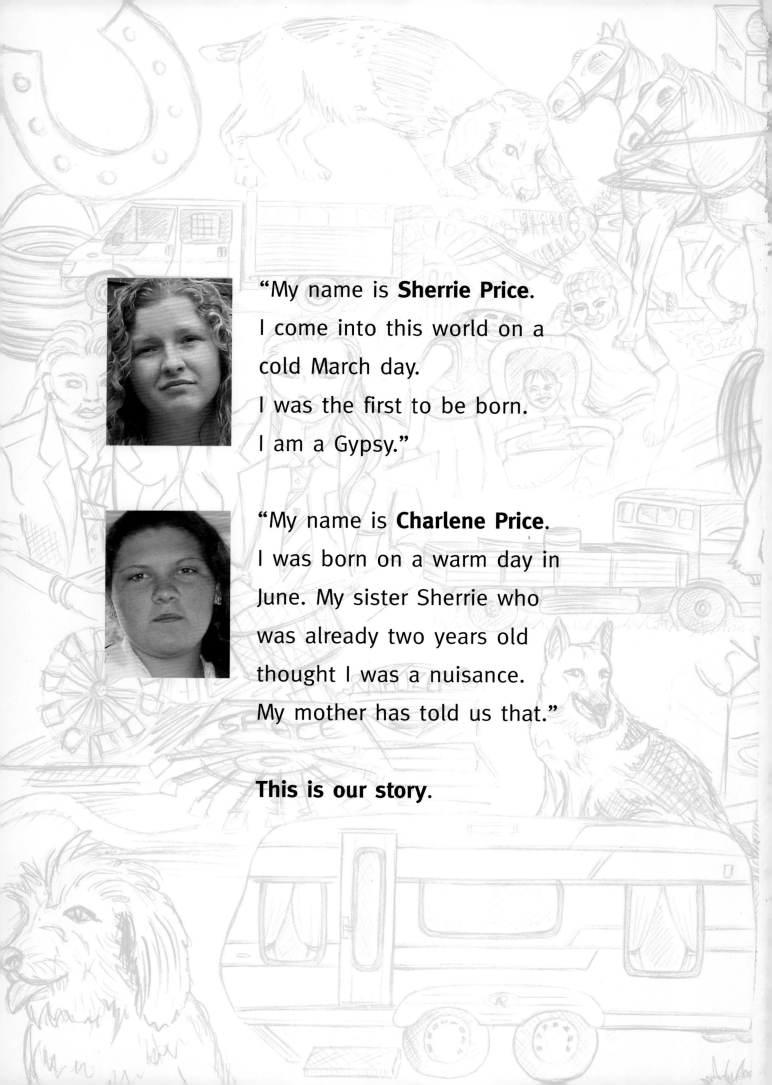

"My name is **Sherrie Price**.
I come into this world on a
cold March day.
I was the first to be born.
I am a Gypsy."

"My name is **Charlene Price**.
I was born on a warm day in
June. My sister Sherrie who
was already two years old
thought I was a nuisance.
My mother has told us that."

This is our story.

Dear everyone

We would like to thank you for taking the time to read our book. We have been researching and gathering information over a two year time period.

We hope you enjoy our book, as we have enjoyed putting it together, to help you have a better understanding of a Gypsy's way of life.

In this book we sometimes use the word '*Gypsy*' and sometimes '*Traveller*'.

We are both Gypsies because we are descended from Romanies. Some Gypsies like to be called Travellers because in the past people used the word Gypsy as an insult. Not all Travellers are Gypsies, for example Irish Travellers. The culture we describe is that of Gypsies.

By **Sherrie** and **Charlene Price**

Our home, a permanent site in Essex.

About me...

**My name is Sherrie Price.
I came into this world on a
cold day in March.
I was the first to be born.
I am a Gypsy.**

My first word was dad,
my dad was so pleased
that dad was my first
word.

**My first day at Felmore
Primary School.**

As my mum took me into
class I started to feel
scared. Mrs Thompson
welcomed me to the class
and then my mum left me. I
felt all alone and still a bit
scared but the other
children came up to me and
I made lots of new friends.

One day I sprained my ankle
and had to be piggy backed
to the car and go to
hospital. I was pushed in a
wheelchair but my mother
couldn't drive it and kept
hitting me against the walls,
God knows what the doctors
thought of us that day! Then
the next day my sister went
shopping, I was not
impressed because I
couldn't go!

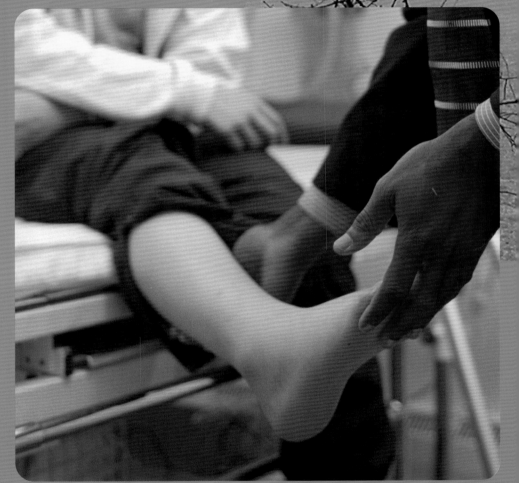

I have three pets which are two
dogs their names are Tyler, he is
a boy dog, and Daisy is a girl
dog and I have some gold fish
in a bowl.

I have two sisters and have a
baby brother. Their names are
Charlene, Lacey and K.J and of
course there is me, Sherrie.

Charlene   Lacey   Sherrie   KJ

When I was first told that I was going to start going to secondary school I was staying in Wisbech for the summer 1999. My Granny phoned one afternoon with "the good news," I was starting in September. I was expecting this to happen but still felt nervous. Now I knew it was really going to happen but I decided to try not to think about it until September.

The school was very big so I feared I might get lost and I actually did get lost a couple of times, as I got confused about the time table.

In the morning the teacher used to meet me at the gate and walk to my classes, even then I lasted only a week and I had a home tutor help me with my studies. I carried it on for two years.

Then it was time for my sister to start school so I had to come, as the excuse of being alone had become out dated. Then a week went by, as you can guess this time, Year 7 and Year 8 and Year 9 weren't as bad as I thought, they were good and I admit I had fun. Year 10 has been the best year.

I plan to get into work with children, so some course work is related to that.

My favourite teacher is Mr Thompson because he is kind and I like his lessons.

My future
In my future I would like to be a SureStart day care assistant. I would like to get married to a Gypsy man far far in the future, and some day I would like children. I would like to still move around but I would like to find a permanent place to live, somewhere familiar. I am not ambitious **I just want to have a happy family life.**

About me...

My name is Charlene Price. I was born on a warm day in June, my sister Sherrie who was already two years old thought I was a nuisance.

Sherrie was born in March my mother has told us that.

Being born in different places shows a bit of Travellers' lifestyle because we were born in different places and different months because in the summer my family used to move around.

In my family there is also my sister Lacey who was going to be called Chantilly but we decided to call her Lacey. She is nine and my littler brother K.J is two.

I have always lived in a trailer. I first realised that not everyone is a Traveller when I was five, that's when I first started school. When I started talking to the other children I was talking to them about my trailer and children said "What are you talking about?". That's when I first knew not everyone is a Traveller.

My family have always had animals we have dogs, chickens, rabbits and horses. We don't have the pets in the trailer because they smell.

The good things about being a Traveller are you get to move around and meet new people and you get to see different places.

The disadvantages are that there are some people who call Travellers names such as gyppo. People who say this are ignorant.

When I first knew I had to go to secondary school I said I won't go. My mum said I have to go.

The day came so I got dressed and my mum dropped me and my sister off. It wasn't that bad because Mrs Blaney put my older sister in my year and my classes so that was alright. I'm in year 10 now and school's not that bad, I can read and write better now.

If I didn't come to school I wouldn't have been able to write this book, so now I have something to be proud of.

I think it's a good thing coming to school. I think I'm lucky because no one has called me names such as gyppo though other Travellers get called names sometimes, and some even get picked on or bullied. I think it is because other people don't understand about Travellers. I think that's why gaujos (Romany word for non Travellers) treat Travellers different to other people.

When I knew I had to go to school I didn't want to go, because all the other Traveller girls and boys didn't have to go so I thought "Why do I have to go?" I said to my mum and granny "It's not fair why should I have to go to school?"

My granny said "Don't look at other people look at yourself." So I said "I'll go but I if I don't like it I won't go no more," so I went and it wasn't that bad. In the past Travellers wouldn't send their children to school, as time went past Travellers started to send their children to primary school. Nowadays a lot more Travellers send their children to secondary school. I think it's because the older Travellers know how hard it is not to be able to read and write.

In the future I think a lot more Traveller girls and boys will attend secondary school.

This is Mrs Blaney with Eastenders Actress who plays Zoe Slater being presented with an award.

About school...

Chalvedon School and other experiences by Sherrie Price

In English our teacher is called Mr Thompson there are only 15 kids in our class and it is a two year course.

One piece of coursework was "Of Mice and Men" written by John Steinbeck; it was very good.

Mr Thompson read the book to us, the class, and then we all got on with our course work about "Of Mice and Men".

Then we did "Romeo and Juliet" by Shakespeare, we read the book and we watched two of the videos one old, and one new one.

We also each wrote an autobiography on ourselves; that was good because me and Charlene used some of our book to help us.

Now the class are working on reading a book called "Lamb to the Slaughter" by Roald Dahl as an introduction to writing a story which can be about love, horror, ghost or murder.

Our story is about horror. It was good even though I don't like writing stories.

My art teacher is Mr McCall. I'm doing a two year GCSE course. I really enjoy art you can have a laugh and still get on with your work.

In art we have studied some artists like Paul Klee, then we put our work in a similar style to Paul Klee. When we were looking at Paul Klee we looked at his work and talked about what things he used like paint and watercolours, and we did the same with ours.

After that we picked a different artist and then picked a theme. I chose 'fashion', other people picked 'celebrations'; that's what we're doing now.

Laptop

I borrowed the laptop from the school. They said to me you can take it home for as long as you need it. I used the laptop to learn my driving theory. So I took it home and learned it every night until my test, which I passed in May. I passed first time! It was great to be able to learn it on a laptop because I couldn't concentrate reading the theory book.

Amy

In Art we both sit near Amy, who is a gaujo. She is very good at Art and we all get on well together

My work experience was at SureStart as a crèche worker. On my first day I went on a trip to Marsh Farm with Jan who is the organiser of all the trips.

The second day I went to the SureStart Centre and worked with other members of SureStart and parents. I met these by going to "Bumps and babies".

I found all the people nice and friendly so now I go back as a volunteer. I enjoy doing baby massage classes.

About school...

Chalvedon School and other experiences by Charlene Price

In year 10 all pupils have the chance of having two weeks work experience in the local community through the Trident scheme.

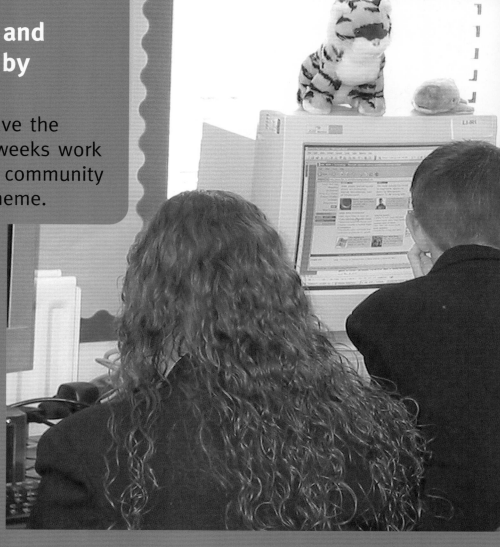

My work experience was as an Assistant Site Manager for Essex County Council. My position was working with the Gypsies living in Essex. I worked with Ann Lee who is the Senior Site Manager for various sites.

On my visits we had to make sure everyone was alright and had no problems. We would then ask if anyone needed electricity cards or to pay their water rates. Then we made sure all the sites were clean and tidy. I also got to go and stay in a hotel as

we went on two courses. I got to meet everyone that Ann worked with they were all very nice and friendly.

Sherrie says:

Advice for Traveller pupils in primary school

Don't worry about going to secondary school, it is not as bad as it looks. Whatever people say it is not much different to primary school, it is just a bit bigger.

Advice for teenagers

A girl's life should not just be about cleaning all day long, you

can come to school have a laugh and make new friends.

Boys, life is not like 15 or 10 year ago and work is not like it used to be! So you could come to school and get some GCSEs and other qualifications and you might want to go to college.

Culture

In the school corridors there are three or four display boards which Sherrie and I have done with help from Mrs Urand about fairs, china, weddings, jewellery and funerals.

The idea is that gaujos in school can learn about our culture and it shows we are proud of it.

About the family...

When my mum was younger they used to move around with their family and friends. When Travellers move around they move with loads of people.

Photograph used by permission of Iain C. McLaren

A Gypsy friend. Peachy with Dolly one of her horses. Peachy and her family breed and race traditional Gypsy horses.

I think it's good to move around with your family and friends because if you don't live near each other you don't get time to see them and talk. I also think it's good to move around because you get to see other people and make new friends. I like moving about because I like to do different things and I also like meeting new people.

I also think it's important to go to Travellers' fairs to see our cousins and friends. We don't always get to see them a lot because they don't live near us. So going to Travellers' fairs gives us a chance to see what they have been up to and where they have been.

I also think Travellers' fairs help to keep the culture. The reason I think this is because the atmosphere is different to other places. Also at Travellers' fairs there's horse selling whereas there isn't at normal markets or fairs. Also people are friendlier at Travellers' fairs. At other places people look at you differently to other people. At Travellers' fairs you can buy different things like Crown Derby, mink hair bobbles and baby's clothes. So I think Travellers' fairs are unique, different from other markets or farmer's fairs.

Photograph used by permission of Iain C. McLaren

Appleby Horse fair circa 1956.
Photos by: Renshaw

Peachy's family at Appleby Fair washing Dolly in the river Eden.

Everybody is part of a family

I think Travellers and gaujos are not that different in some things but in some other things they are very different.

For example gaujos are part of a family. They include mum, dad, brother, sister and their granny, grandad, cousins and also close friends.

Travellers spend a lot of time with their family, where I think gaujos don't spend as much time with their family as Travellers do.

Gaujos don't really see their cousins. I think they don't really class them as family. Whereas Travellers do. Travellers class them as family and spend a lot of time with them.

If our family or cousins don't live close they will always meet at fairs like Cambridge fair.

I think gaujos only see their distant family at weddings or funerals.

Most of the family live near each other but the ones that don't always meet at fairs or weddings. Travellers always try and see each other as often as they can. My grand parents live in Sheffield and we go down there 10–15 times a year, we also see them at fairs and weddings.

In my opinion Travellers are a lot closer to each other, than gaujos. I also think Travellers spend more time with their families, than gaujos. I think with us Travellers, we like to live around with our families and our cousins.

Clever girls...

Travelling girls are clever because when they want something doing, like if one of the girls wants something doing with their motor they'll just say, "Will you do it for me?"

For example changing the oil or changing the tyres.

The boys won't make a fuss they'll just do it. The boys will do it because they can. Most of the boys learn these things like mechanics at an early age from their dads.

Jobs are different now because when the men were younger they used to do field work like apple picking

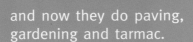

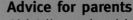

and now they do paving, gardening and tarmac.

When I leave school I would like to get into beauty and health care.

If you are not like them, some people put their noses up in the air because they think they are better than you. That makes me cross because we are all equal.

One of the problems is that not so many Travellers go to school so people don't learn that they are the same. I think coming to school helps people understand.

When I was in primary school my friends came to my place and I went to theirs.

Advice for parents

Girls' lives should not be the same like cleaning all day long; they will get bored. You can go to school, it is a laugh and you can make good friends.

I know what you are thinking, "There are only gaujos at school" but if some of your friends and family go, there will be some Travellers too!

Boys, life is not like it was 10 or 15 year ago, today you will need GCSEs and more qualifications to get work.

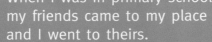

Best of friends
cousin Florie and Charlene.

Jewellery and Fashion

Most of the young Gypsy girls don't really wear the big bulky gold earrings any more they tend to wear more delicate things like little diamond studs and things like that.

Nowadays gaujos girls tend to wear the big gold earrings (I think it is they're just trying to act like Travelling girls!). A lot of Gypsy girls don't really wear a lot of silver but sometimes they do. I think it depends on what else they're wearing. Gypsy girls like wearing diamond rings, big or little. I think it is because they're just nice.

I think most Gypsy girls do have big gold chains but they don't really wear them. I think they wear them around horse fairs. But I think they wear more delicate necklaces around Cambridge Fair, I don't really know why. Gypsy girls don't generally buy silver chains and rings I think they like having gold and gold is something you can keep for years and silver just gets thrown away. I think it is mainly based on what they wear, sometimes they might wear silver but mainly they wear gold and diamonds.

Family get togethers, Appleby and other fairs.

Appleby Fair is the fair that most people have heard of. Appleby is in the north of England so it is a long way.

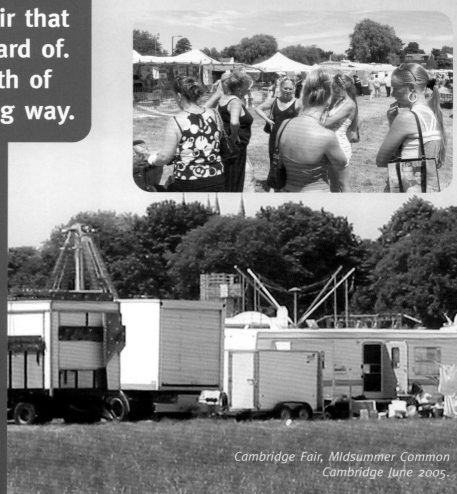

Cambridge Fair, MIdsummer Common Cambridge June 2005.

It is a traditional Gypsy fair with lots of horses, stalls and horse trading. People take old wagons.

The horses race down the road, it is dangerous.

They wash the horses in the River Eden. They also have trolley racing.

Appleby Horse fair circa 1956. Photos by: Renshaw

My family live so far apart so we meet at some fairs like Cambridge. Cambridge has a big fun fair there are some rides and there are some stalls that sell Crown Derby and no horses are allowed.

Watton is a horse fair and somewhere you can buy Crown Derby. Fairs have always been important for Travellers.

Sometimes the family will all decide to meet at Hunstanton. Hunstanton is a beach near King's Lynn where we spend time picking seashells, swimming, burying each other in the sand and eating fish and chips, having all sorts of fun all day long.

Royal Crown Derby
I am 16 years old and I buy Crown Derby. I have a little job to pay for it. I buy mine from places like Cambridge Fair.

These are some of the pieces of the china I buy. Some of younger Travellers buy Crown

Royal Crown
Derby plate
and Shire Horse.

Derby too. The girls are more likely to buy than the boys. When they get married, if the girl wants Crown Derby the boy will buy it for her. Many Travellers collect fine china. Some collect Aynsley and some green panel. It is kept in a cabinet to look at.

Lacey's story....
When Travellers move all the china has to be wrapped and packed away. Lacey watched her mum packing the china away. She was only four at the time.

She wanted to help so she started putting Mum's china on the bed. My mum saw her and was surprised Lacey was even touching the china but fortunately nothing was broken.

Girls and boys, weddings and funerals...

Most of the Gypsy girls and boys go out with each other at the age of 17 or 18. The boy always asks the girl's father if they can go out.

Most Travelling girls and boys meet at Travelling fairs like Cambridge fair or weddings and when they go out with all the girls and boys.

A Gypsy couple.

They mainly meet at big get togethers like the conventions. If they wanted to get married the boy would ask the girl's father if they could get married (and her father would always say YES.) Then they would have a big wedding and all the family would come, all the friends and the cousins and any one else they know.

Photo: Sally Penfold
A Gypsy wedding circa 1911.

Marriage

The bride and groom will get ready in separate trailers. It is unlucky for them to see each other before the wedding. The bride will usually travel to church in a horse and cart. China is always given as a gift to start their married life. All the families gather after for a party. Travellers usually marry Travellers but sometimes Travellers marry gaujos. Young Gypsies are allowed to go round together in a couple from about 16 years old. Young Travelling girls sometimes marry around about 18 years old but some girls like to have a life before they are married, like going on holidays.

Weddings

Weddings are big things for Travellers because everybody goes from all over. All the family and friends, cousins and any body else they know. It's something all Travellers' children look forward to and all the young girls and boys like going because it is a time where they all get together and meet people they haven't seen in a long time.

Travellers' weddings are always a big event for the young girls and boys because it's a time for them to buy themselves some new clothes and things and the girls love buying new clothes any excuse!

Gypsy Wagon with children dressed for wedding party circa 1921.

Burning of a Gypsy wagon after a funeral ceremony 1947.

Also the mothers and fathers like going to weddings because it also gives them a time to catch up with people they haven't seen in a long time or sometimes years.

Funerals

Gypsies' and Travellers' funerals are the same as non-Gypsies and Travellers, the men will sit up all night, that's to show their respect to the person who died and the women make tea and coffee for the men. Sometimes the women might sit up but normally they sit in the trailer.

Most of the old Gypsy men and Travelling men would own their own horses and carts, so most of them would be tacking to the church on their horse and cart. Gypsies and Travellers would always have big horse and cart wreaths made, or something else they like, but it would always be big.

Gypsies and Travellers' funerals are always something everyone knows about and Gypsies and Travellers would always make a point of coming even if they came from the other end of the country (if they know who died). Even if they didn't know them, that will show their respect for those who died.

In the past Gypsies burned the homes that the deceased lived in; it was usually a wagon. This rarely happens now.

About places to live...

My mum moved more when she was younger. Now if you move around you get moved on by the police but when my mum was younger the public didn't really bother with Travellers. Today there are some people who are prejudiced and some who are ignorant of the Traveller lifestyle. Also the law makes it difficult to move because they have made it a criminal offence to stop on the side of the road.

Nowhere to stay.

A country lane blocked with concrete and rubble to stop motors getting in.

Some people class all Travellers the same as the ones that cause trouble, such as dumping rubbish, starting fires and children shooting at windows with a catapult. So when you move on a field or car park they might give you one night then you have to move. Sometimes they might let you stay for a few days or they might tell you to move the same day. If you don't they will take action.

Today if you buy ground the council often won't pass planning applications. I know Travellers this happened to. Sometimes trailers (caravans) get towed off and the fences pulled down with a bulldozer. The children cry and mothers worry about how they can keep their children safe and give them an education. It is very frightening to hear about this because I wonder what it would be like for me and my family to have nowhere to go.

I think it is even more difficult for Travellers as most of the older Travellers can't read or write. Sometimes they do not live on a permanent site and they are unable to get help.

In the past, a hundred years ago people had wagons and horses and there were lots of places to stop. Most people have wagons and horses for show now. Then Travellers had trailers and motors but still moved around.

When my granddad was a young man there were lots of green fields to stop on. People let you stop and gave you water. The farmers had lots of work.

By the time my mum was born there were sites and people stopped sometimes but also travelled. Now there aren't enough sites and you aren't allowed to stop. By the time you have unpacked they ask you to move on. Also there is not much farm work because the farmers have sold the ground to build houses! The farmers don't need so much help.

In the future they might make us all live in houses! That would be awful.

Sometimes people are ignorant of the Traveller lifestyle and this can make fitting in difficult at times. Traveller parents are suspicious of secondary school, often because of the size and in case the children will be looked on as second class citizens. I think they might be right because I have personally experienced an incident in which a teacher made me feel lower class. It started because I wouldn't pick paper up because I didn't throw it. So he kept me in and let everyone else go. I don't think it was because I was a Traveller but that is because I think that Chalvedon School does acknowledge Traveller's culture.

Newspapers
I think that sometimes newspapers are not fair to Gypsies and give a prejudiced view but at the same time, some try to be fair and help Gypsies and Travellers. I have written to the papers myself agreeing that Travellers do need more sites.

You would never guess what happened! In March 2003 my baby brother was born at 11:55pm. He was the first boy because there are three girls.

A lot of Travellers do not breast feed. They don't like to show their bodies and as they often travel to large fairs it gets awkward. Also there is very little privacy in a trailer.

So they bottle feed because it is a lot easier. When they are walking around fairs they can just get the bottle out and feed the baby.

Travellers Health

An old Gypsy proverb says Gypsies value three things: freedom, health and love. For without freedom there can be no health and without health love cannot be enjoyed.

Health problems amongst Gypsy Travellers are between two to five time more common than in the settled community.

Because Gypsies travel around, it is difficult to get registered with a doctor and Gypsy sites are often situated next to dumps, so this can increase the spread of disease. Pregnant Gypsy women can suffer illness or miscarriage due to the fact that they do not always receive proper ante-natal care.

It is not true that disease amongst Gypsies is spread by bad hygiene, they are very particular about cleanliness.

Trained health service staff should be available to treat Gypsies, without the ignorance and prejudice that is around today.

Cleaning

The girls clean. We have a bucket and wash leather to wipe inside and out for the trailer and sometimes a washing shed. The girls do most of the cleaning but sometimes the boys are made to help to clean.

Toilet

Some people think we don't have a flushing toilet, well we do. We don't have to dig a hole

in the ground like I think some French people still do today.

Pets

Travellers have different Pets from gaujos. Travellers have chickens, running dogs, trotting horses and birds such us goldfinches but gaujos tend to have birds such as budgies. Where gaujos have ponies, rabbits and cats, Travellers hate cats because they smell and carry germs. Some Gaujos even have animals like cats and dogs in their home, all over the kitchen.

Why are jobs different nowadays?

Jobs are different now because when my mum and dad were younger they use to do field work like apple picking and now they do paving, gardening, tarmac.

What do men do mostly?

Men mostly go to work, come home and some of them go to the pub. Some might help with the cleaning but not very often. Most of the men can mend motors. The men do help with the children but mostly with the boys.

What do women do?

Most of the women don't go to work, they just clean up and when the men come home they might go out or the women will cook.

Will young Travellers keep the same type of work?

I think the young Travellers would like to keep doing what they are already doing now like paving and tarmac. People will always want roads and paths, so they will never be out of work. I think some of the young Travellers would like to go to college and learn paving and get qualifications and also some might learn how to drive a digger. Many of the girls do marry young and don't go to work but some don't get married young and do go to work. I think people are surprised how clean we are because they think all Travellers and Gypsies are dirty and smelly but we are the cleanest people around. All Travellers clean their homes every day they don't just quick flick with a duster, they clean top to bottom.

Old times...

There was a time when I was seven and my sister Sherrie was nine and my aunt Louise was eighteen.

Louise and Sherrie were sunbathing and I was sitting in the trailer.

I kept messing about and kept saying "There's a dog coming" but there wasn't. I looked again and there was a massive dog coming, so I told the girls but they wouldn't believe me so I went back in the trailer. When the girls saw the dog they started screaming. I was in the trailer and I couldn't stop laughing. Then the farmer came and took the dog back. Sherrie and Louise were going to kill me! That was at Wisbech.

Sometimes the family will all decide to meet at Hunstanton. Hunstanton is a beach near King's Lynn.

In the summer my uncle came down so all the men and women went out for dinner. My youngest sister Lacey was in bed, my sister Sherrie was sitting in the trailer door. Me and my aunt Louise had the bestest laugh in our life. We took me dad's brother's motor and messed about skidding in the field. After, we couldn't get the motor in the same place as it was, so we had to go and get the farmer's boy to put the motor in the same place we got it from. And from this day they still don't know not unless they read this of course!

One fine day at Wisbech

Wisbech is a little village near King's Lynn. We lived on a big field but now it is a housing estate.

It reminds me of a hot day when my mum took my aunt Louise to the town. When she left, a big white horse come running down the field. The farmer who owned the horse came running after it. He was very worried in case a car might hit his horse. I was in the trailer with Charlene when the trailer moved and we heard a horse galloping. We were surprised but realised a horse had got loose. It could have been dangerous and could have hit the trailer. This could have hurt the horse

Hunstanton Norfolk

but my mum would have said that the trailer would have been more damaged.

This is like Wisbech but it is not the same place because the field is a housing estate now.

In the future they might make us all live in houses!
That would be awful.

New housing development.

All about using this book...

As teachers we can see many ways in which this book can be used with pupils across the Key Stage 2 and secondary school curricula. It can also be used with staff for cultural awareness training and as part of the general library resources for everyone's enjoyment.

Here are just a few of our ideas.

Learning about:

- Romany Gypsy culture and traditions

Exploring:

- identity and diversity
- equality
- prejudice and stereotyping
- the meaning of respect

Discussing:

- similarities and differences between people
- lifestyles, families
- rites of passage, weddings funerals and celebrations
- people and their animals
- leisure time and hobbies

Increasing understanding of:

- aspects of economic and social change
- people moving and settling
- changing patterns of work
- how the law affects individuals and groups

Talking about:

- transitions between home and school, primary and secondary school, school and work

Using as a stimulus for:

- writing for an audience
- writing with a purpose
- autobiography
- writing an account

Kanta Wild-Smith Essex and Southend Consortium Traveller Education Service
Barbara Blaney Head of Learning Support, Chalvedon School, Basildon

This is a year that Sherrie and Charlene can look back on with considerable pride. Two weeks ago Sherrie was among our Year 10 Prefects welcoming 330 new pupils to the School. Last week, highly commended by their teachers, they both received awards on Presentations Evening. However, Sherrie and Charlene are aware that their success is unusual – the odds of succeeding in the education system are stacked against Gypsy Travellers.

These two young ladies knew that they had an important story to tell. Their target audience is diverse: Travellers will be encouraged by their achievements, non-Travellers will gain an insight into their culture and identity, and schools will see how they were included without any pressure to abandon their traditional way of life.

Their appreciation of and affection for their teachers is mutual. Sherrie and Charlene have blossomed in a school that celebrates cultural difference and appreciates that all pupils are individuals with special needs.

On Presentations Evening I told our pupils, "Have pride in your heritage; know where you came from, and be proud of it. Learn about your roots – your background, your family, your school." Sherrie and Charlene make the same point here...but so much more persuasively!

Alan Roach
Head of Chalvedon School